First Steps in Reading

Reproducible Activity Sheets for Grades K-1

Troll Associates

Troll Teacher Time Savers provide a quick source of self-contained lessons and practice material, designed to be used as full-scale lessons or to make productive use of those precious extra minutes that sometimes turn up in the day's schedule.

Troll Teacher Time Savers can help you to prepare a made-to-order program for your students. Select the sequence of Time Savers that will meet your students' needs, and make as many photocopies of each page as you require. Since Time Savers include progressive levels of complexity and difficulty in each book, it is possible to individualize instruction, matching the needs of each student.

Those who need extra practice and reinforcement for catching up in their skills can benefit from Troll Teacher Time Savers, while other students can use Time Savers for enrichment or as a refresher for skills in which they haven't had recent practice. Time Savers can also be used to diagnose a student's knowledge and skills level, in order to see where extra practice is needed.

Time Savers can be used as homework assignments, classroom or small-group activities, shared learning with partners, or practice for standardized testing. See "Answer Key & Skills Index" to find the specific skill featured in each activity.

ANSWER KEY & SKILLS INDEX

Circus Parade

monkey   zebra   giraffe

The  is **first.** Color it brown.

The is **last.** Color it yellow and brown.

Name_____ **Date** _____

1

Line Up!

Color the **first** animal yellow.

Color the **last** animal brown.

Name_____   **Date** _____

At the Carnival

Who is **first** in each line? Color that person orange.
Who is **last** in each line? Color that person blue.

Name_____ **Date**_____

3

On the Move

Which comes **first?** Color it red.
Which comes **last?** Color it green.

Name_____   Date _____

Circus Friends

Color my hat **black**.

Color my tie **yellow**.

Color my coat **red**.

Color my pants **blue**.

Color my boots **green**.

Color my hat **blue**.

Color my nose **red**.

Color my buttons **black**.

Color my pants **yellow**.

Color my shoes **green**.

Name _____   **Date** _____

5

Connect the Dots

Who's the tallest animal in the zoo?

Connect the dots to find out who!

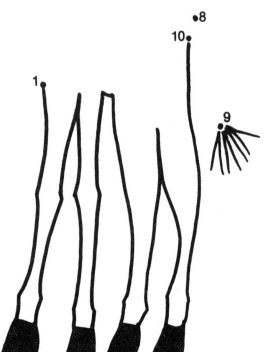

What's Missing?

Draw in what is missing on this rabbit.

Name_____ Date _____

Hooray for Hippos

How many big hippos are here? _____

How many little hippos are here? _____
Color the big hippos blue. Color the little hippos yellow.

Name_____ Date _____

Walrus Pool Party

How many walruses are in the pool?_____

How many are not in the pool? _____

Color the ones in the pool orange.
Color the ones out of the pool blue.

Name_____ Date _____

A Sunny Day

Who is in **front?** Draw a circle around him.
What animals are **behind** the farmer? Color them yellow.

At the Circus

Who is **inside?** Color them orange.
Who is **outside?** Color them yellow.

Name_____ **Date** _____

11

The Train Ride

Who is **inside**? Color them orange.
Who is **outside**? Color them yellow.

Name_____ **Date** _____

Around & About

If he is **over** something, color him blue.
If he is **under** something, color him yellow.

Playful Balloons

Which balloons are **over**? Color them blue.
Which balloons are **under**? Color them red.

Name_____ **Date** _____

Around Our Neighborhood

What is moving **toward** you? Draw a circle around it.
What is moving **away** from you? Draw a square around it.

Name_____ **Date** _____

Here's the Circus

Who is going **away** from something? Color them red.
Who is going **toward** something? Color them yellow.

Name_____ **Date**_____

16

Yummy, Yummy

Color the things that are **full**.

Name_____   Date _____

17

Playtime Fun

Which things are **empty?** Color them blue.
Which things are **full?** Color them red.

Name _____ **Date** _____

18

Who Weighs More?

The big hippo or the little hippo? _____

The big panda or the little panda? _____

The big elephant or the little elephant? _____

Name_____ Date _____

Circus Time

Draw a circle around each **small** thing. Color the **big** things.

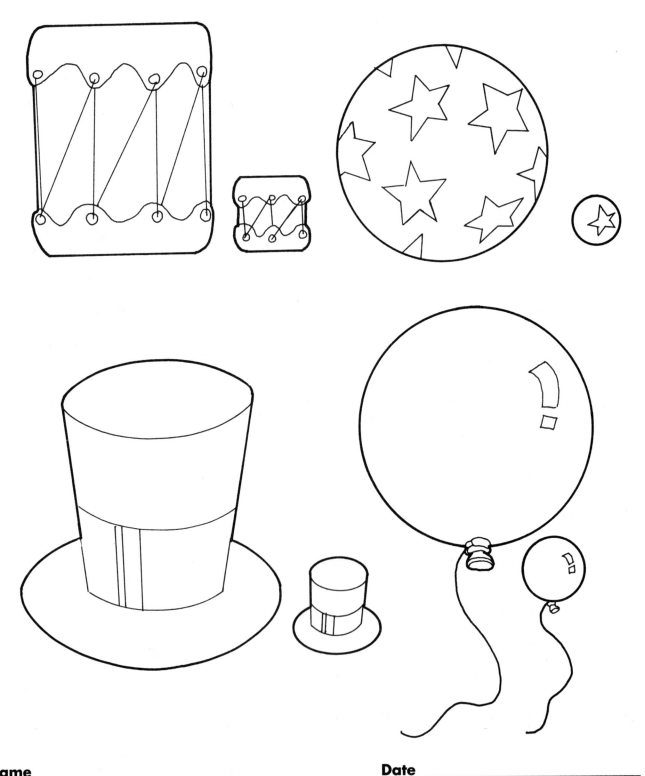

Circus Animals

Color each **big** thing. Put an X on each **small** thing.

Time for the Show

Circle the smallest one in each row.

Name_____ Date _____

Circus Acts

Circle the largest one in each row.

Name_____ **Date** _____

23

Size Wise

Number these animals in order from smallest to largest.

_____   _____   _____   _____

_____   _____   _____   _____

Name_____   **Date** _____

Up-Down Playground

What things are **up?** Color them yellow.
What things are **down?** Color them green.

Name_____ Date _____

Hip, Hip, Hooray

Which are facing **front?** Color them orange.
Which are facing **back?** Color them blue.

Name_____ Date _____

Circus Fun

Find the **long** things. Color them green.
Find the **short** things. Color them orange.

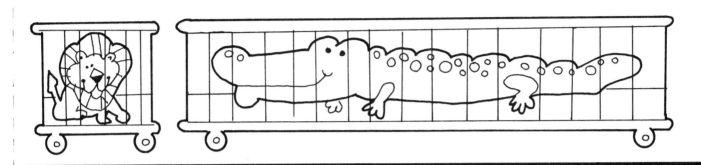

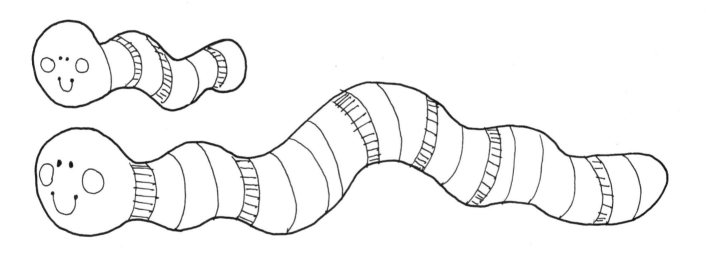

Name_____ Date _____

27

A Funny Time

Color the **tall** things. Circle the **short** things.

Name_____ **Date** _____

Rainy Day Riddle

What goes up when rain  comes down?

Color the picture that answers the riddle.

train

sun

umbrella

Cut out the correct picture and attach it below.

ATTACH
HERE

Name_____ Date_____

29

Circus Stars

Color the people or animals that are **on top of** something.

Circus Clowns

Find the ball that is **nearest** to each clown. Color it red.
Find the ball that is **farthest** from each clown. Color it yellow.

Name _____   Date _____

Monkeyshines

left	right

Color the picture on the **left.**

Color the picture on the **right.**

Name _____ **Date** _____

Jumping Clowns

Which clowns are on the **left?** Color them yellow.
Which clowns are on the **right?** Color them red.

Name_____ Date _____

Millie & Max

left	right

Look for the boxes that say

left

Color them **blue**.

Look for the boxes that say

right

Color them **red**.

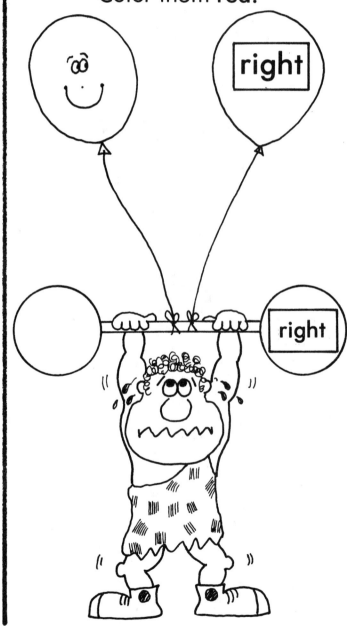

left

left

millie

right

Side Show Sillies

Read the words under each picture. Then cut and attach.

Put me on
the **left.**

Put me on
the **left.**

Put me on
the **right.**

Put me on
the **right.**

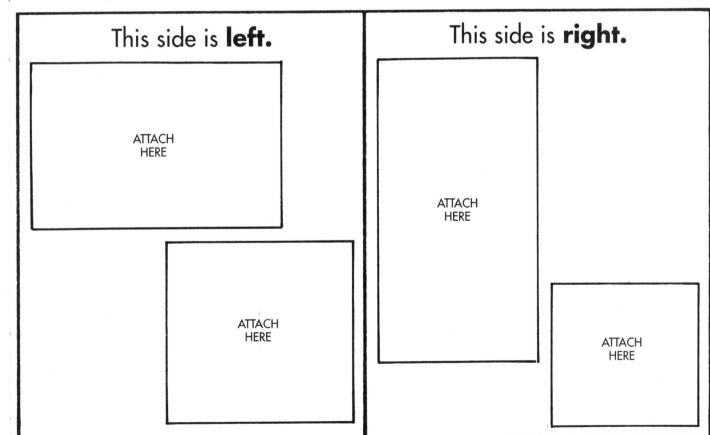

This side is **left.**

This side is **right.**

ATTACH
HERE

ATTACH
HERE

ATTACH
HERE

ATTACH
HERE

Name_____ Date _____

Toy Animals

Which animals are facing to their **left?** Color them blue.
Which animals are facing to their **right?** Color them yellow.

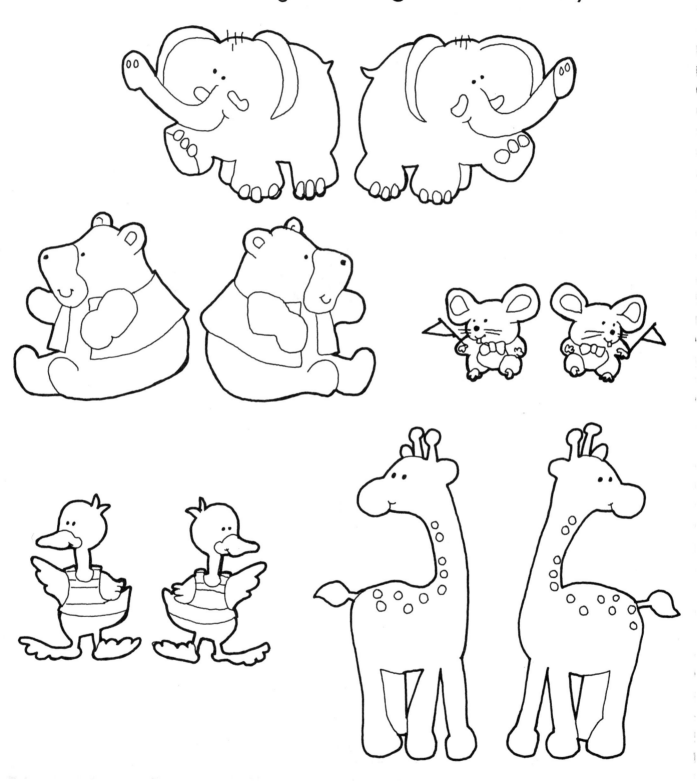

Name_____ **Date** _____

Party Time

Joe is going to a party. Help him find his way.

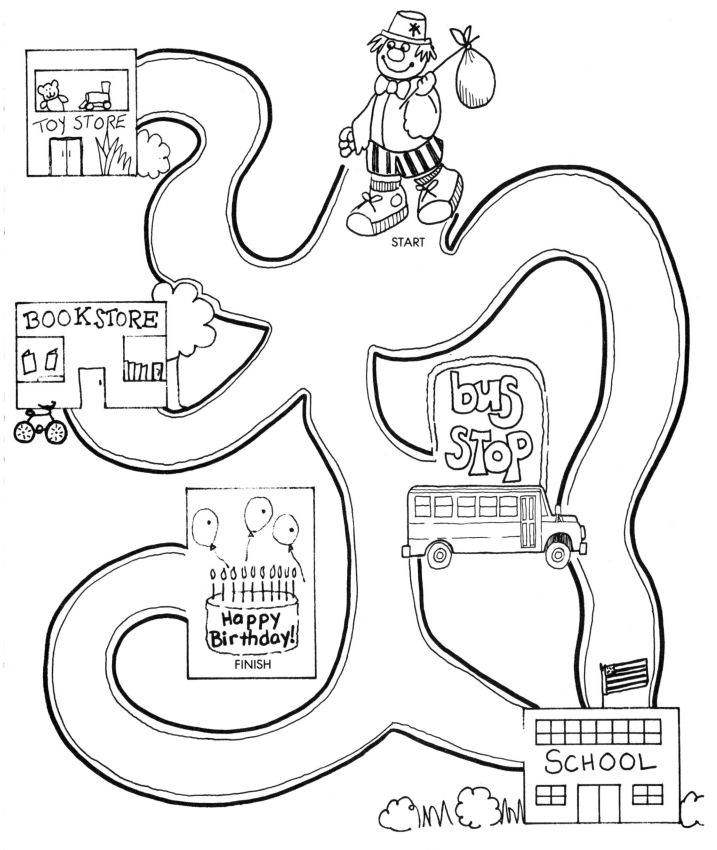

Lost Little Panda

Help the baby panda find his parents.

START

FINISH

Name_____ Date_____

What Doesn't Belong?

Circle what does not belong in each row.

monkey

bus

banana

tie

elephant

peanuts

hay

drum

horse

Name_____ Date_____

Same & Different

Place an X on what is different in each row.

 # X Marks the Spot

Place an X on what is **different** in each row.

Name _____ **Date** _____

41

Just for Fun

Color the things that are the **same** in each row.
Put an X on the thing that is **different** in each row.

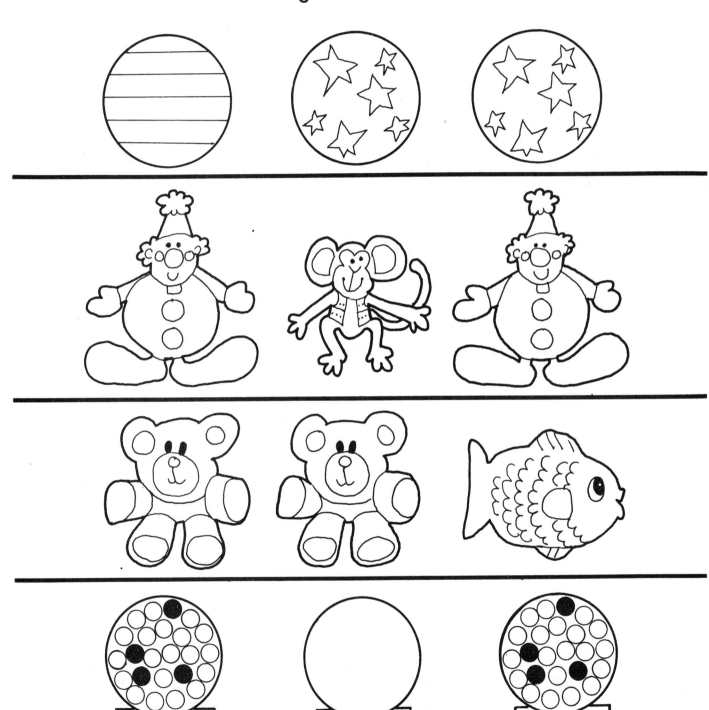

Find the Twins

Color what is the **same** in each row.

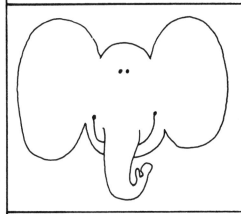  

  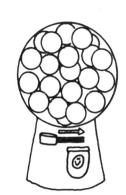

Name _____ **Date** _____

43

Two's Company

Color the two objects that are the same in each row.

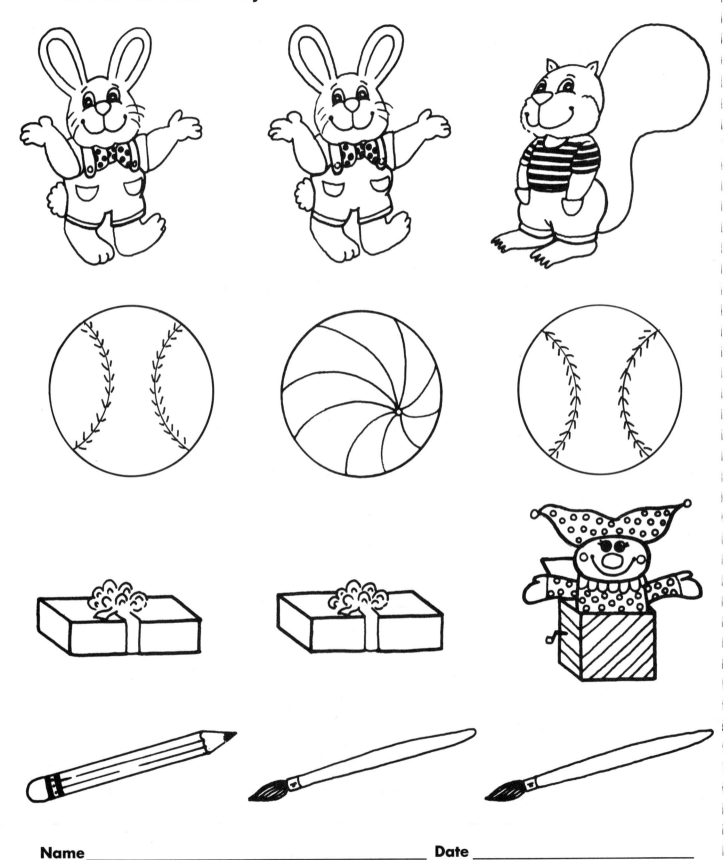

Name_____ **Date** _____

What's Different?

Color what looks different in each row.

 # Look-Alikes

Color what is the same in each row.

 # What Sticks Out?

Color what is the same in each row.

Time for Tricks

Put an X on the one in each row that is not like the others.

Name_____ **Date** _____

Copyright © 1996 by Troll Communications L.L.C.

Something's Different

Place an **X** on what is **different** in each row.

Name_____ **Date**_____

49

Find the One

One letter in each row is different. Circle it.

a   a   d   a   a

* *

s   s   s   t   s

* *

r   r   r   r   x

* *

i   l   l   l   l

* *

c   k   c   c   c

* *

m   m   n   m   m

Name_____ **Date** _____

Meet Mighty Max

Put an X on the letter in each row that is not like the others.

c   c   o   c

t   k   k   k

b   b   b   d

n   m   m   m

Name_____ **Date** _____

51

Three-Ring Fun

Put an X on the word in each
row that is not like the others.

fun   fun   run

tent   tell   tent

bear bear bean

Name_____ **Date** _____

52

Word Search

Two words in each row are alike. Circle them.

1.   you   fun   you   tin   are

* *

2.   to   is   as   is   of

* *

3.   car   the   hit   pig   car

* *

4.   new   let   bag   new   ape

* *

5.   as   he   it   so   it

* *

6.   dog   cat   rug   cat   bird

Name_____ Date _____

Charlie Chimp

Help Charlie Chimp put the 3 letters
in each row in alphabetical order.

1. E B D
2. P N M
3. Z W X
4. J H K
5. W V X
6. T Q S

1. ___ ___ ___

2. ___ ___ ___

3. ___ ___ ___

4. ___ ___ ___

5. ___ ___ ___

6. ___ ___ ___

Name_____ **Date** _____

Who Lives Here?

Cut out and attach these zoo animals in the correct cages.

CUT HERE

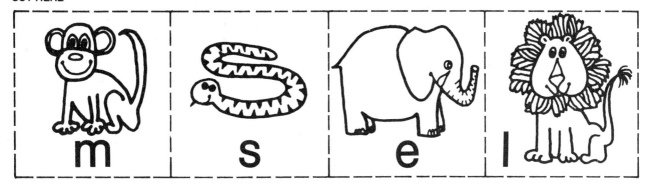

m   s   e   l

elephant

lion

snake

monkey

Name_____ **Date** _____

55

Alligator Adventure
Help Albert find Alvin.

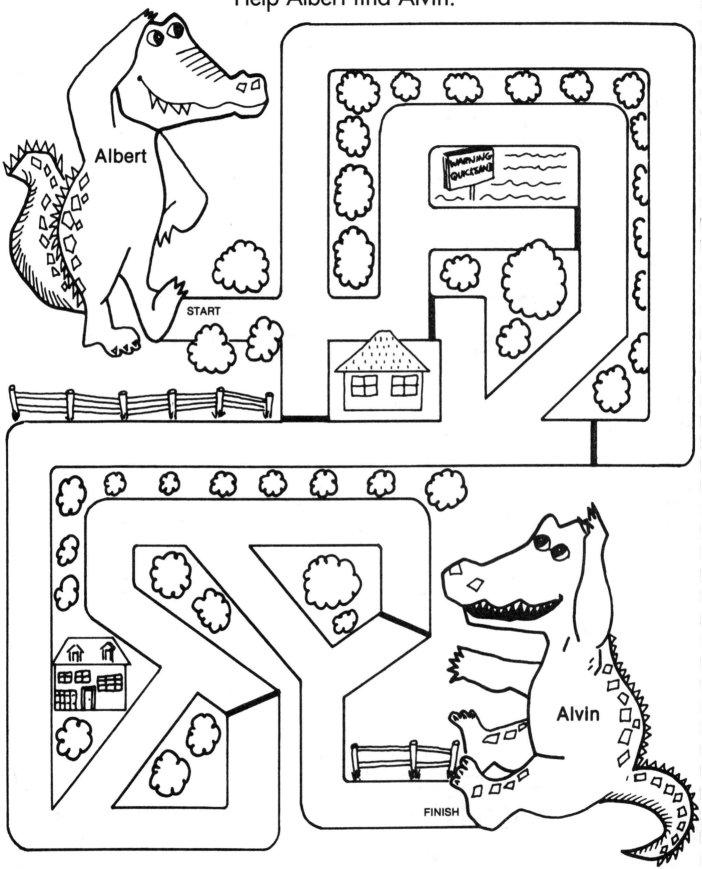

Name_____ Date_____

Missing Vowel

The same vowel is missing
from each of the words below.
Fill in the blanks.

e a

o i u

o

m__use   z__o

b__ok   n__se

__ut   li__n

Name_____ Date _____

Kangaroo Kazoo

What does this kangaroo have in her pouch?
Write the first letter of each word on
the blanks below to find out.

____ ____ ____ ____
book apple boy yellow

____ ____ ____ ____ ____ ____ ____ ____
kite ant noodle grape art rake out or

Color the picture.

Leo's Trick

Look at the words in the box. Circle the **first** word.

jumps	sits	eats

Now write that word in the space.

The _____ .

Now color the picture that
goes with the sentence.

Name_____ Date_____

Rhyme Time

Circle the word that rhymes with
the first word in each row.

book	hoop	hook	boom	take
bat	hat	hop	hit	but
make	mark	cart	cake	cook
sun	food	fin	tune	fun

A Pet for Pete

Look at the words in the box.
Circle the **last** word.

ball	bike	bird

Now write that word in the space.

The ____ has a _____ .

 Now color the picture that
goes with the sentence.

Name_____ Date_____

Something Fishy

The first letter of Sam's lunch is "**f**." Please find it. Color it **yellow**.

fish

cake

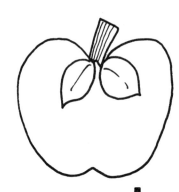

apple

What is Sam's lunch? Write the word here.

_____

- - - - - - - - - -

_____

Name_____ Date_____

62

Showtime for Sam

Sam wants his toy.
The first letter is "**b**."
Please find it.
Color it **red**.

shoe   ball   hat

What did Sam want?
Write the word here.

_____

_ _ _ _ _ _ _ _ _ _ _ _

_____

Funny Animals

Write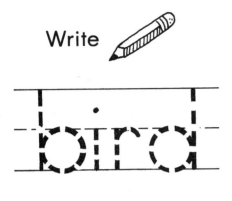

Color the bird **red**.

Write

Color the cat **yellow**.

Write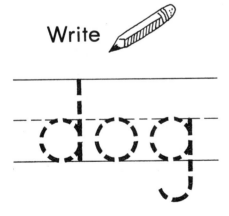

Color the dog **brown**.

Name_____ Date_____

Penguin Puzzle

Color the penguin. Then do the puzzle below.

1. F **2.** I

ACROSS
1. They live in water and penguins eat them.

DOWN
2. Penguins live where there is lots of snow and i __ __ .

Name_____ **Date** _____

Missing Word Mystery

Find the word that goes in each row. Write the
letters in the boxes. The ↓ shows you the way.

hat

nose

hand

shoe

Name _____ Date _____

Lion Puzzle

Color the lion.
Then do the puzzle below.

ACROSS

1. The sound a lion makes.

DOWN

2. The fur around a lion's head.

Name_____ Date _____

Crisscross Words

Find the word that goes in each row. Write the letters in the boxes.
The first one shows you how.

1. | h |
2. | o |
3. | r |
4. | s |
5. | e |

1. horse

2. dog

3. tree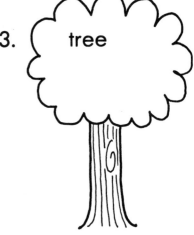

Name_____ Date_____

68

Elephant Opposites

Connect each word in the first column
with its opposite in the second column.

big   down

night   out

in   little

up   day

Name_____   **Date** _____

Word Puzzle

How many words can you make from these letters?
Write them on the lines below.

S	R	T
A	M	I
O	L	E

_____

_____

_____

_____

_____

Name_____ **Date** _____

Scrambled Letters

Unscramble these letters.

dgo ___ ___ ___

gip ___ ___ ___

lwof ___ ___ ___ ___

rbae ___ ___ ___ ___

drib ___ ___ ___ ___

morw ___ ___ ___ ___

rtibba ___ ___ ___ ___ ___ ___

etirg ___ ___ ___ ___ ___

Name_____ **Date**_____

New Words

How many words can you make from these letters?

O	N	P
E	S	Y
I	T	W

Write them below.

Word Bird

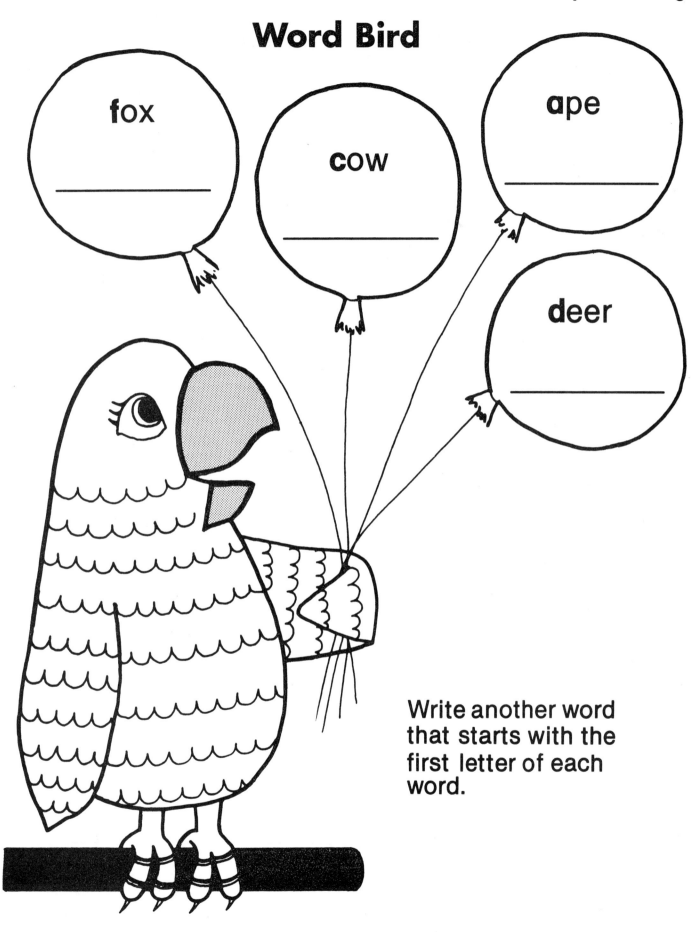

fox
_____

cow
_____

ape
_____

deer
_____

Write another word that starts with the first letter of each word.

Name_____ Date _____

73

Making Words

Make a word by unscrambling the letters.

rca

_ _ _

tiek

_ _ _ _

papel

_ _ _ _ _

gink

_ _ _ _

Lost & Found

Write the answers to the questions on the lines below each picture.

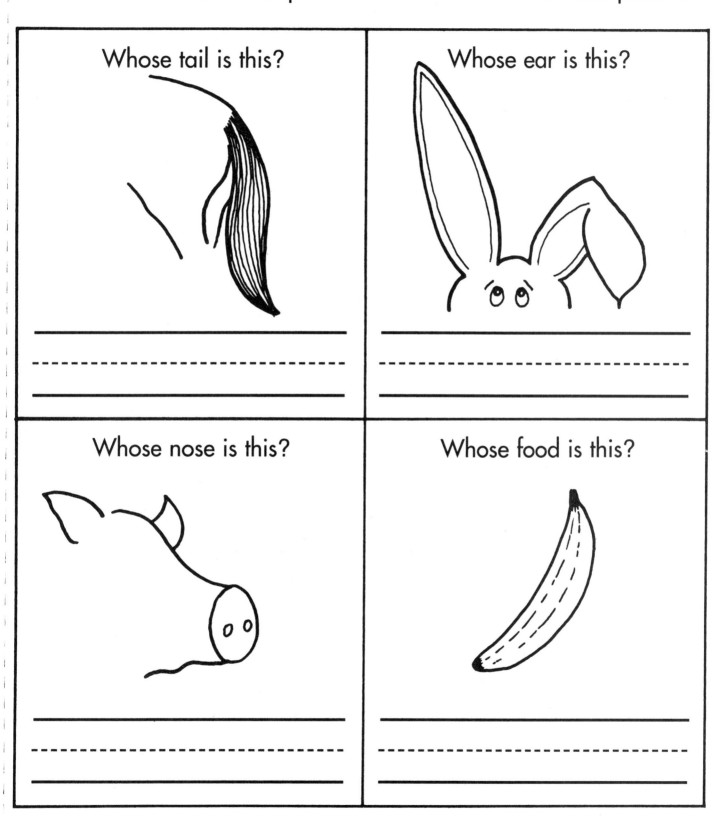

Whose tail is this?

_____

- -

_____

Whose ear is this?

_____

- -

_____

Whose nose is this?

_____

- -

_____

Whose food is this?

_____

- -

_____

Name_____ **Date** _____

75

Solve the Mystery

Write the answers to the questions on the lines below each picture.

Whose house is this?

Whose tail is this?

Where do these wheels belong?

Whose stripes are these?

Name_____ **Date** _____

76